NIRVANA HAYMAKER

Frank Reardon

NeoPoiesisPress.com

NeoPoiesis Press

Inquiries:
P.O. Box 38037
Houston, TX 77238-8037

Primary Address:
2775 Harbor Ave SW, Suite D
Seattle, WA 98126-2138

www.neopoiesispress.com

Frank Reardon –Nirvana Haymaker
ISBN 978-0-9855577-7-5 (paperback : alk. paper)
        1. Poetry. I. Reardon, Frank

Printed in the United States of America.

First Edition

Cover design by Milo Duffin and Stephen Roxborough

Also by Frank Reardon:
Interstate Chokehold, ISBN 978-0-9819984-4-2

for Scott Wannberg & Mike Taylor

"tell the bus driver i meant the next stop
if there truly is one." --Scott Wannberg

Contents

War in Silent Places

my empty
& growling stomach
is the only
real feeling
i need

to remind
myself

about war
in silent
places.

It Stays With You

Charlie Marlow
sat in his
booth
while chomping down
on the all-you-can-eat
pancake special

his tired eyes
glanced into the endless desert
when the horror finally hit him,

"the heart
can only handle
so much"

Sometimes a Magnum .44

Richie,
were you the
bad guy
pretending
to be good

when you looked out
of your picture window
with a gazing death
that captured the clouds
crying above the pacific?

& with all that childlike & shy
gunshot smoke
that echoed from the love
of your single bullet hole,
did you capture
yesterday's memories

& finally destroy
all of the us
that were hiding
inside
all of the you ?

A Letter to Whitey

Whitey,
i know about
taking the
pain & frustration
out on a
punching bag,

one that hangs
anywhere at
any given time
in any given place,
town or city

i know about
hitting it
over & over
with a confession
of strictly trained
muscles,

pulverizing it
until the idea
of running
is no longer
an option,

until the skin
of my knuckles
becomes the skin
of yours.

i know all about
being the champion
of where ever
you're standing,

knocking out
the inner
sociopath with
mean & brutal
uppercuts,

the crowd
standing &
roaring
our names.

Whitey,
i know about
family,

& i know how
to slam
a pint glass
across someone's
forehead
just to
protect them,

then, after,
with blood
on my hands,
giving the victim
faith tips
on how to use
the first bead
of a rosary.

Whitey,
i know how
hard it is
to pretend
that you're
someone else,

wearing masks
& disguises,
telling stories
to keep
the heart safe.

i understand
the small victories
& how to save them

by placing
them in your
breast pocket,

using them
later just
to show the
world that you
are more
than
nothing.

Whitey,
i understand
that murder
is not only
for the roses,

& i can feel it
when their colors
are boiling
the bones of
my eyes,

& i know
that when
i am caught
i can show
the world my
cocksure smile,

but when it is time
for me to confess
everything
that i have done

& the gods are
ripping out my guts,
exposing me
& throwing their wrath
upon my
grave by means
of electricity,

you can be sure, Whitey,
that i will never
give up my beliefs
or friends.

All the Discarded Rinds
of Your Paperplate Soul

when the women of the world
have left you alone
in your bed
staring up at the ceiling
because
you could not afford
anything other than
that one can of beans
in your cabinet

when she told everyone
that you knew in your lives together
that you were pathetic & weak
because
you could not afford
anything other than
that one beer
someone else left
inside your fridge

when she fucked your neighbor,
best friend, or biggest enemy
because your ATM card
was declined
while buying cigarettes

just know
that you are
the luckiest man alive

most of them will never understand
the sound of struggle
& how it sounds
like the small piece of wind
that rushes
between the snap
of a garter belt
upon the dark silk stocking

most of them cannot comprehend
that it is a gift, struggling,

a sexiness,
that makes love
to the discarded rinds
of your paper plate soul.

Set Your Idols on Fire

When
the ticks &
jitters
try to
become
one,

they rub
together
like
red phosphorus
& sulfur,

igniting
one lonely
flame
inside
the dark
hand
of who i
am,

it is
the only
way
to
shorten
the lines
& remove
the
lies,

it is
the only
way
to set
the idols
on
fire,

it is
the only
way
to free
insanity
from
desire.

Punch the Clock Before It's Gone

some people
are born
with their eyes
unopened

and it's easier
for them
not to see

they'll ask you,
"hey did you
see that?"

or, "can you
fetch me my
glasses so
I can see
that better?"

and when
they have
to use their
own sight

they'll get
angry
and moan
when they
have to strain
themselves
to take
notice

they'll accuse
you of stealing
if it's not
right in front
of them

they'll give up
if they have
to look

for themselves

they don't
want to be able
to see
and i cannot
blame them

i can see, but
then again...

Only a Few Can Dance Across the Milky Way

do you
think
you are
brilliant
because
you
know
the names
& colors
of all the
flowers?

try to
understand
what
makes
them
grow.

Muse: Downtown Crossing

when i was looking at the mirror
she was behind me on the bed,

      ribbons of naked splendor,
      long flows of smoke   falling
      on undependable ash floors.

she dressed herself in
                    rigid flames
     & archaic rhythms

as she followed me out the door
    into Jamaica Plain particulars,

onto Orange Line,
where script kings dealt in death
      with seats of lonely purity,

where old men bewildered in memories
of Grace Kelly & Spencer Tracey,

where goodbye travelers noticed clumps
of Centre Street on soles of blood clot.

 she watched
        as elegy for John Coltrane
        as hollowed out skull
        as waged war against time.

stepping onto Downtown Crossing platform,
i headed past tunnel trumpets
& voices lost in foot patterns.

she moved as long stroke of brush,
flowing behind head full of ecstasy.

into spring air, outside station,
    people banged cobblestones
    police rode leather saddles
    death trembled on hard nipples
    lovers mused as angels of sexuality.

from behind,
she grabbed the crook in my arm
& we walked as two psalms in search of parables,

      exploding god rhythms
      onto the lethal limits
      that lay in the cement.

we blew kisses into devious symbols
      on Winter & Washington St.
we hustled cheap soft dough pretzels for 2.99
      in front of Jive piano boy
      of Jordan Marsh dollar hat.

Park Street gospel boys handed out pamphlets
to the end of the earth.
Gilchrist rappers stared down
heroin addict Boston Common.

she was a path past livid devil from great fire ghost,
& i spoke softly into my own spit
as we fucked in a funeral line.

her love was a parade of gestures,
    a juice dripping from a strange face showing the natural.

she was something
                of the barbarian
coming
into thought

          by which the theory
          of difficulty

    in being the self,
               was us (erratic invitations

& as we sat
on J.J. Foley bar stool
(21 Kingston St.
          smiling into foam rings & cosmos,
          conducting internal investigations,

celebrating the functions
     of long passageways
       into echoes of confusion.

& i pawed at her tits,
     moving my hands
     up & down her meaty hips.
it
was
universal,
       plucking the flower
          of the muse.

The Endless Sky Above the Suspension Bridge

let us break our necks, or at least write
a Japanese death poem,
but let us not be the lightning lying helplessly,
for it's nice to look up from the ground at bridges,
or so a ravaged doll once said, it feels impulsive,
and impulsive carries a lot of weight,
more weight than myself,
we should like how it feels when embankments absorb us,
with their thickets of cold muck
and endless hours of calm, but comfortable boredom,

up high, as high as the broken bones can see,
i know that there are long lost kingdoms
inside the cables of a suspension bridge,
the ones from the other side of the sky told me so,
and the gods have become jealous of my gaze,
especially Apollo, because he cannot understand
why the sun is so fixated with my pale face,
neither do i, it's wet, grimy and it's missing its strange voice that
was lent to me by my father's depression and alcoholism,

such is the song of all that has passed,
i'm solemn here, and utterly for the taking,
soon i expect the city to take me away,
far away into their lonely histories,
they'll perform a ceremony or two,
someone will light a candle, whisper something profound,
they'll comb my beard and drain my blood, such is the song,
such is the dullness of boring men and their soundless pity,

the answer to your question won't be found here,
i like your urgency too much to give it to you that easily,
but if it was not for your inquiry i probably
would have not found peace,
peace in bodily fresh spasms and tortured swelling,
i have often wondered, if i did give it to you
would your mouth become pregnant
with charming and sensitive mercies?
would you try to turn beauty
into something contrived with marketability?

O, how Basho must have felt when his family
moved into his hut and asked him so many questions, teacher's
guilt is hell, Oh, never mind,

i like to watch the cars up on the bridge,
the trucks, bikers and walkers,
where are they going? can they see me at all?
do they notice the goodness and particulars around me?
do they see the angels with their checklists and instructions?
can they see the Mississippi
and its hopelessly romantic river weeds
reach from the fog like old river devils
stealing my hanging ribs?
there is so much they don't know in their infinite hurry,
O, how i love to know that i can feel the blaze in between,
with its glorious colors and stillness of perfect melody,

let us be our own realities and live in them so tightly
that not even the wind from a shitty epitaph could find us,
let it sound so indecent that it would make
the sheets of St. Millay blush,
and like all afternoons down at the bottom of velocity
i dare mention the story
my friends from the wilderness once told me,
they said: if you drop a penny off the empire state building
it would gather so much speed
that it would crack the sidewalk,
or blast a hole the size of a moon crater into someone's head,

i was always amazed by that, and i often wondered if beautiful
Eden's and marvelous poetry would finally
seep out of the holes in their heads,
i wonder if the travesty of crap that disarms
a man's ordinary life
would pour from their holes like an unstable magma,
like an uncontrollable fire with a burly chest
that is finally pushing them around after being trapped
for so long,
and as i lay here in intricate and different shapes,
unlike my former shapes, of marrow, blood, saliva and bone,
gasping the last of this earthen fuel,
i'm inclined to believe it.

Windowsill

i don't know how to close the shades

kids are outside the window playing handball
with a loud bang
while above me the light of jazz blinks from last week.
What else can i do?

The cigarette laughs at the warmth of my coke bottle
while the sweat drips into the sounds of my lungs.
Groaning in front of the fan,
i used to, but who cries anymore?

The street lights are not much lonelier than myself,
long tall trumpeters of Centre Street,
strong and elaborate in their needs, blue with feeling.
They've got hands that i can almost see. They play tricks
with what the street grates only know, almost, but not yet.

i can see the boredom of the trash, back and forth,
forward and back, but these feelings of mine are not ill.
Ask the shapes of the trees and notice how they've aged.

The old lady sings to her cat.
Her voice is an eviction notice that used to sing.
i admire that. The cat does not.
He jumps out onto the porch, almost happy,
and in confidence with his tail, he looks up at the stars.

With belly aching, and a promise to the gods about next week,
not this week,
i am almost me.
i am almost cured.

The last of my aggression captures the stars.
i am not myself.

i am the last of the war meat.
Not the first. Not the blues, but always true,
like the way that woman's heel clanks up the hill,
always her heart at 4 a.m. in the mist
of a stranger's wrist watch.
Her aches are beyond what i see

in the back thigh lines of her nylons.
They seem to be the counter weight to my pulley.
Am i drifting toward it? Am i not?
Maybe yes for certain. This coke is good.

There is something infinite on this windowsill,
something perfect like the absolute feeling
of stupidity and strength.
i am infinite too, almost persuasive,
almost all done with the moon.
My infinite apologies to you, sun, for hiding
while you were trying to rise on the other side of my head.

If it's all the same to you, i'll sit here a little longer.
i'll remember the Ave Maria you sang to my grandmother.
i'll watch for the eager notes you leave on the side walk.
Follow you?
Maybe, just maybe, but
i like when the moon is racy.

People Are Too Bored To Die

avoiding
people
by
being awake
& alive
at 2am

is what
some
would like
to call
my cry
for help,

but as
i sit
under
the stars,
lifting up
the skirts
of constellations
& kissing
that
last
breath
of wine,

i know
that this is
my cry
for
life.

Some Are Afraid of the Pain

She asked me, How do you write a poem?

Come on over here to my desk,
help me take this bear trap off my heart,
& i can show you.

Bear trap?
I don't see a bear trap around your heart!

Then why are you asking?

When You Least Expect It,
It Will Smash Into Your Locked Door

he had flown
into the
door
& snapped
his neck
or spine

so, i shoveled
him up
& placed
him in a
peaceful
spot

between
two trees
& on top
of lush
green
grass,

& through
his one
good eye
& from his
twisted
body,

the
dying
bird
said:

how
does one
handle
all of
this love?

10 a.m. Valiums

Debbie would wake up every Sunday morning
raising hell with a Saturday night hangover.

She'd scream at the newspaper sections
that were out of order,
carefully placing the crooked corners back into shape.

"God damn lazy pieces of shit," she'd whisper,
her hands still trying to place the corners
of the newspaper sections back in perfect order.

After 10 a.m. coffee she'd go straight to the bathroom,
pop two Valiums into her mouth, and swallow.
Then she would pour orange juice and champagne
into a glass.
Two or three drinks later, the Valiums would kick in.

Debbie would throw her arms around me,
give my 16-year-old face soft kisses & say,
"I'm so glad you came out of me. You're a good boy."
Then she'd push me away and smoke a ton of cigarettes.

By 1 p.m. i was helping her to bed,
Debbie, still in her bathrobe from the morning,
her hair still a wild-fire-red-mess.
She'd fall on her back laughing
as i threw her legs up on the bed
and pulled off her slippers.

"I might be still married to your father
if he fucked me half as good as my uncle did."

"Sure, Mom," i would say,
putting a glass of water
& two Valiums on her night stand.

Stomach in a Bag

i carry my stomach around
in a plastic grocery bag.

All
the
way
down
the front
of the bag
it says "Thank You"
in big red letters.

Inside is the vomit and the acid,
the harsh realities
of what punches and kicks can do,
of what makes me human.

They always look on as i dip
my hands into the bag and pull
out random books and begin to
read on the side of the road.

Lighting a cigarette,
i just stare back into the sun that turns the dark sky pink.

In the corner
on the ground
my stomach sits in a bag,
ripping and growling into the Minot wind.

It wants to chase the onlookers.
It tries to move,
but it just flutters,
holding itself together
because it is weighed down by its contents.

Instead of committing murder,
it just stares and says, "Thank You."

As time goes on,
every day

i pull out
and place things back in.

i hang it on hooks,
close steel locker doors on it,
stuff it into cabinets,
step on it,
throw it into the garbage.
i let fruit rot inside.
i let it grow holes.

Sometimes it blows away,
flying high up into the sky,
but it always crashes down
and hits the ground.
It always growls and rips,
always tries to get back up,
fighting fiercely.

Most days
you just have to accept
that there are no longer
any legends,

not the kind that
expose their stomachs,
not the kind that carry
empty bags.

The Most Beautiful Red Head in Town

She would get her tears in order
while putting on her makeup in front of the mirror.

She'd carefully paint fire engine red lipstick on her mouth,
puckering kisses into the void,
as her hips swayed to the record she told me to play.

Her fire red hair flowed onto her blouse.
Her wool skirt hugged her hips & landed mid-thigh.
Meeting the bottom of the skirt were black stockings
clasped gently & trying to make promises.

She'd dance a small spin in front of me
acting as if i was the only audience in the world,

"How does mama look?"
"You look like a princess," i'd say.

After pouring another glass of straight gin,
she'd always play Ruby Tuesday
& pick me up
& dance me around the room.

We would sing the song together, out loud.
i'd make her laugh because i would mess up the words,
so she'd dip me into a huge messy kiss,
my nose & cheeks covered in her lipstick.

Then, like always, the doorbell would ring.

She'd quickly put on her heels
& begin marching towards the door.
She went from mommy to sexy in the blink of an eye.

Another man with a mustache,
another man in a denim shirt,
drooling all over himself,
grabbing her ass as she went for her purse.
They'd always smell like beer.

"Frankie, there is cereal in the cabinet."
"Okay, Mama," i'd say,

staring at her as she lost eye contact with me.

The door would begin to shut on the porch light
& i'd feel the darkness of the door
close, its heavy weight & fury
upon the light inside my heart.

Words Like Talons

Debbie's fist went through the screen door
while Frank held me in his arms.

"That is my son, you manipulative mother fucker,"
 Debbie screamed.

Her red flew all around the front porch.
As it jumped around from her skull
it blocked the sun from my eyes.

Her boots kept kicking the metal door.
Dent after dent she made as her eyes cracked yellow.

"Let me the fuck in, you asshole," she screamed.
Debbie's purse kept slamming against the door,
finally ripping down the entire screen.

Frank opened the door to save himself
from embarrassment.
They both sat down on opposite sides of the living room,
myself standing in the middle,
looking back and forth at them.

"Come here, Frankie," Debbie said,
pulling up & fixing my pants,
planting kisses on my forehead.
i just kept looking at her,
frantically rubbing my toy truck
that i was holding in the grips of a nervous sweat.

"Come over here, big guy," Frank said.
i ran over to him from my mother's embrace.
He showed me a Whiffle Ball & bat.
"Later on we can go play in Grandma's backyard."

i smiled & held the glory of the yellow plastic bat
high up in the air,
swinging it around the living room with all my little might.

"What a piece of shit you are, Frank," Debbie yelled,
picking up my toy truck & throwing it at his head.
She stuck out her tongue at him & gave him the finger.

"You cunt-hole!" he yelled.

The words flew back & forth
as i stood on my Grandmother's green carpet,
still in the middle of them,
looking back and forth,
my toes digging into the carpet's softness,
like talons,
ready to attack.

Linoleum Prison

She'd clean until the pain was gone,
scrubbing every corner 'til she sweat.

She'd grind her teeth as hard as she could,
crazy eyes & drool pouring from her brow.

Toothbrush after toothbrush would turn brown,
her wrists would swell up and pop
as the corners of the floors began to fade.

"Can i have lunch?" i'd ask.

With hands in tremble she'd sneer,
"Not until I'm fucking done! There's dirt everywhere."

i'd look into the floor
and all i could see was the glow of my face.

Vacuums,
mops,
a strange array of cleaners,
(each one serving a different purpose)
tons of rags & old torn t-shirts.

With each job, each purpose,
she'd work the heart of her hands,
over &
over &
over,
she'd clean all the things she already cleaned.

i'd sit and watch,
"You asshole! You lazy asshole! Go outside or do something!"

She would then pause
as if the music in her head had ended,
and she'd rotate around the room in panic,
(hands still moving the tooth brush furiously
on the cracks of the wood.)

Standing up,
off balance,

32

she'd run to the bathroom,
going to the place of her pink colored pills.

i would sit in a chair in the middle of the room,
all the furniture gone for cleaning,
the sun shining through the windows
making the floors glow like thousands of oak candles.

From the bathroom
i'd always hear her crying,
wailing like a dying dog
in the middle of her sparkling linoleum prison.

Roselle's Morning

Roselle could not lift up her feet in the morning.
Her slippers shuffled across the floor like a train.
She'd wince through her arthritic condition,
because her feet were swollen like two small ripe-red fruits.

Making it to the kitchen,
Roselle would pop two aspirin & percolate the coffee.
She'd use two hands on the counter to remove her weight,
breathing heavy because she knew it was her duty
to get everyone out the door in a good mood.

"Good morning," she would say to anyone,
whether their faces were covered in piss,
whether or not they had plans to commit murder.

When the hordes of the ungrateful made their way out,
Roselle would sit in her chair & turn on her tiny radio,
her head bowed to listen to the priest speak.
Her face went from tensed to elevated within seconds.

"Holy Mary, Mother of God, pray for us sinners
now and at the hour of our death. Amen,"
she'd whisper, over & over.
Her only movement was each arthritic hand
massaging the other.

It had her in a float above the physical pain,
above the spousal abuse,
above the affairs.
It gave her the strength to choke death & live.

The Hail Mary's flowed from her lips
like flamenco guitars
that had gone completely out of control,
or like tiny rubies of blood
in full dance pouring from her mouth.

When the priest was finished,
Roselle would turn off the radio & walk over to the sink,
pouring a glass of water & drinking it
as if she was at a bar.
She'd stare out the window

34

watching the birds fly around the backyard,
watching the squirrels steal the bird food.

Her pale blue eyes would begin to slit
tighter & tighter as she exclaimed,
"Those damn squirrels are bastards!
 They never respect anything!"

The Ball Breaker

My father wore his uniform proudly.
He'd march around the apartment
shouting orders into the air at no one.
He'd look at his stripes in the mirror,
the drill sergeant,
the ball breaker,
but the mirror exposed him every time.
The long lines on his face
were no longer a threat to anyone.
He was missing teeth.
His eyes drooped.
They no longer had wit,
class, or intimidation.
His bright blues would grow cold & pale
like a slow Chopin concerto
that made the cat run from the rain.
It would always be with this realization
that the ball breaker,
the great drill instructor of commandos,
began to take it out on everyone else.
He'd sit silently for a moment in his chair,
(uniform still perfectly pressed.)
He'd look over at me reading books
or writing poems.
His eyes would snarl.
They'd say to me, silently,
"No faggot son of mine!"
Then the table was flipped,
and i was slammed against the wall.
After a few slaps,
after a few breathy orders shouted into my face,
he'd reach into his pocket and pull out a 20,
forcefully slamming the money into my sweaty hand.
His hand closed my hand onto the money,
my fist becoming purple as he squeezed harder & harder.
He wanted me to accept the cash
without any word,
as his eyes still dared me to make a move,
as his last few teeth still clenched,
as he breathed heavily into the mirror,
looking at himself,
begging himself

to take orders from himself.
But those stripes,
those
god
damn
stripes,
were
so
fucking
hypnotic.

Black Chinese Dress

Devonshire St.
feet pounding   *with*
        mind sex & other observers,
        with lust & sunny spectator secretions,
you'd channel the lips of the universe
in a music selection from your head phones.
        with   nothing to *lose*
            & nothing to *gain,*
you'd hold onto the fragments of my heart
  in your hands
  like a bouquet of flowers
        that waited
                patiently
within the urges of your body,
        wrapped tight, shining
            & battling against
                    electric-red-dyed-hair
convulsing with my raging desire
        to unzip   your
                        Black Chinese Dress.

The Oak Park Four

Souris River

i crack peanut shells in the fog of Souris River.
Beady eyes on the ground stare at me.
i whisper silently into their furry gaze.
i too know a thing about hungry winters.

In Passing

You climb on the bench with me, crunching rapidly.
My mind is clear as i continue to look forward.
You ask without words, "Why are you still here?"
"My heart is calm," i answer, putting down another peanut.

Peanut Money

i sit in the car with nervous shakes, drinking beer.
The nine-inch family looks at me from the parking lot,
looking for my indifference to float into the void.
"i spent the peanut money on beer you fuckers!"

In The End, Count On Yourself

The birds have flown south for the winter
& now everything is dead, brittle, & crunchy.

i sit with the cold mountain inside of myself
until only my freezing breath remains.

Gaining Wisdom

Janice & i
toured the Jamaica Plain bars
mid-day, laughing &
trolling Centre St.,
alive & beautiful.

We'd be as silent as Buddha
while sitting on our old stools,
sipping from cheap brown bottles.

She leaned her chin
onto her meaty hand
as she sighed through her boyish face.

I think I'd like to be with a guy, next time, she said,
shifting her thick thighs to an uncrossed position.
I wonder what a nice, stiff cock would feel like?

Through the corner of my eye,
i took a peak at her butch lesbian features.

Well, Ah...Maybe... i thought to myself.

She reached into my pack of cigarettes,
pulling one out. My hand rose to light it.
Janice & i always moved & spoke nonchalantly.

Stiff cocks are not all that, i told her.

No, really, I want a nice hard one.
I wanna get fahhhked so hard that I feel it in my throat.

i chuckled a bit, sucking off the last swill.
Janice moved her ass up the stool,
exposing the crotch of her black panties.
Yeah! That's right! I wanna get FAHHHKED, real good!

Pussy is where it's at, stick with that,
don't complicate your life, i replied.

She moved her hand onto my thigh, rubbing it
as she ordered us two more of whatever would go into a cup.

Hippo, you wanna be my first cock?
She always called me 'Hippo' when drinking.

i looked forward into the bar mirror.
It was mentioning some sort of advertisement.
The lines on my face were heavier
& there was no longer any life in my eyes.

Feed me that BIG Irish load of yours, Hippo.

She kept making proposals
with new sex demands each time.
i kept looking into the spaces & pieces of my face.

Fahhhhhk off Hippo, I'll find another who wants this ass!

Gazing into that mirror's advertisements,
i finally discovered all of the traps
& gained their wisdom.

Knocking Down Towers of Blocks

i was the middle one of three,
but i was the only one who made it.

The first ended up in a toilet.
My mother
waved goodbye & flushed him,
his face the color of yolk,
little eyes asking "why"
as he went in circles down the long hole to nowhere.

The last
rose like a fresh loaf of bread in her stomach,
(there was a brief reconciliation between my parents)
but he became controlling.
She made a doctor appointment.

Afterward, for a few days
she walked around the house like a zombie.

i'd be building blocks & she'd shuffle through my tower,
knocking over my perfect stacks of 1, 2, & 3.
Sitting down at the table,
she poured some coffee & stared out the kitchen window
running nervous hands around her abdomen,
beginning to laugh & cry at the same time.

i gave her the block that had the number 2 on it.
Holding it in her hand,
she moved her thumb around the blue colored number.
She looked over at me.
Her chin touched her chest, her neck stretched back.
The scream was so loud that the dog howled.

Thin as Blood

They are no longer people
just   thinning curtains
                    to gaze through
Punching on these bloody flowers
i can only see
          unstoppable
                 distances

Lonely Legs for the Stretching

When i came to California
all i could find was
           Robinson Jeffers' leg,
     alone,
on the side of the road.
It was tired from
                running,
tired of chasing after
                nothing.
It had left its mouth
                and tongue,
it had left its lungs & started
a marathon to anywhere.
     Jeffers' one single leg
hopped from Big Sur
                down to NOHO
then collapsed
under palm tree sidewalks,
looking for me
to peel the flesh from the bone
and make my own journey
out of things   all
                       alone.
i used Jeffers'
     old wounded leg
        as a cane
heading down
        Lankershim Blvd.
i looked majestic,
i gawked at ladies
                saying,
"how do you do,"
     with a tip of my hat
& a thump of old Jeffers'
galloping history.
     i tapped the pavement
with the tendons and bone,
knocking out the vibrations
     just to see
           who was there
        before me,
just to imagine

44

                    that one day
my bone
        might be used
          in this long stretch
                        of history.

The Heart Can Shadow Box

O, Louis-Ferdinand Celine, the boys are coming to get me,
to wrap me up in their mighty robes
& rip open my chest full of moonlight, leaking it
upon the blind understatements i clog myself with.

Am i to become the fragrance of curious ecstasy
following around these difficult men with too much talk
and rifles of change in their golden eyes
of boundless heavens?
O, Celine, breast of the fleeting me, entirely,
blue as the sky as if you taught me the legends of French.

i remember the beautiful women in chalk drawings
carrying baby-baskets full of sunny dispositions,
and how they winked at death with those kisses
from old post cards.
My eyes were their virgin birth
        when venturing into the pleasures of their hyacinth,
and i spoke in reds & blues, an alphabet of vowels,
record stores & animal sounds...
 O, Celine, i remember the battles, the raging-indiscriminate
as bedtime became a foreign language of open wine bottles.

Our filth was a mysterious saint, strutting on the streets,
wearing early movie blue jean garb,
        snapping fingers and making love to hydrogen bombs.
Our regret was a meditation behind a door without a knob,
touching the hearts of sidewalk art.
        Love, Love—Oh, the God damn mighty love!
            where i lost the print of my family name,
            where i shared the blade with *war-dogs,*
            where i put my fingers in front of a flashing light
upon bedroom walls, hands full of shadow-puppet-birds.
        O, Celine, the Laughter,
                    the Dreams, the Freedoms.

It was in the powerful gallop of horses that struck me
        inside the cafe, beside that painting of a sad morning,
spilling blood from my eyes, hands, & tone deaf ears,

and i wanted life,
        to live as a knife in the swashbuckler's mouth.

i wanted strength
        to punch into the 15th round.
                Now they only have 10 or 12,
but i want to do things like they used to have them done, Celine.
Holding it all in,
not giving anything away for free,
nothing at all,
dancing,
punching,
& liberating
with every single bit of the insides that i've got left.

E.

Essentially,
i hear
    the   thoughts
of quiet
    as a   sound
with forceful yet
calm flow   of *distances,*

bursting—
    immortal frenzy,
      wonderfully
         tumbling.

The Hunger in London

When the Klondike cried
        with its loud golden bells,
    it was a little too loud for your ears,
 but it pulled hard
   with the midnight arms
                of a sweet lady,
& you growled like a wolf
         drenched in the hunger
      of *icy snow.*
 & as you stood in the fires
                of early morning,
   you noticed that the dust in your mind
had become
        the ashes

Air Shaped Doors

The *out most* margins, natural
    in your decision not to love man,
you only wanted to feel the Pacific's wings,
        organically
     within a midnight's
          flicker-spray
of salted lips that cracked the skin
     & penetrated the progress of anguish.
It had to be done
    in front of holy diversions
      while creating intricate ideas
by the severed hand
        with a supreme capacity
to build a stone-hawk-tower
    out of *the emptying darkness.*
Those were the long nights
     shouting poems, alone,
   trying to discover
       those *air shaped doors.*

Unfinished Quivers

Timid little animals
   with big *Gothic* eyes
carry human afflictions
   deeply
within the tapestry
   of their   *bones*
as a living collection
     of unfinished quivers
   torn between
typewriter
     & unrest

 & when you stopped *shaking,*
    God tried
        searching.

When You Don't Pat the VIG

"oh...oh...OH NO! Call an ambulance...Jesus, No!"
is all i could hear
as my eyes
fixed in on my uncle Jimmy
like a zoom lens
in a movie,

he was shirtless
under a pile a leaves,
they had tried
to set him on fire
but somehow the flames
had gone out,

his arm,
exposed with its tiny shamrock tattoo,
was hanging out
from among the mess
of dirt, sticks, & gasoline coated leaves,

his eyes
were meaty pulps of beefsteak,
running down his cheek,
the lines of blood
had carved out his
facial structure
with tiny pieces
of dirt traveling in between,

"uh...uh...OH NO!...is...is...he ALIVE!"
Get that kid outta here!"

an unknown arm had grabbed me
tightly around my chest,
trying to pull my away from
the scene of the crime,

the paramedics came
& they did not pull the sheet
over his head
so i knew he was alive,

back at the house
my grandfather
was making phone calls,
opening his safe
& stuffing
big money into envelopes.

Go Fifteen With the Typewriter
Before the Gods Ring the Bell

It won't smile at you
before landing
a haymaker
keep on your guard
keep the gloves up at your chin
& learn how to counter
with all of your might
wisdom & courage,
if you don't
you'll never be able
to go toe-to-toe with it
because it dances the mat
with a mighty fury
jabbing
crossing
hooking
leaving you bloody
& lifeless.

if you can go toe-to-toe
with it
you need a lot of stamina
because if you
can keep up
you'll be dipping & punching
with concertos
weaving & upper-cutting
with the heavens
& if it goes down
for the count
it will only be
because you
learned to throw
the most
beautiful punches
the world
has ever
thrown.

Falling Down a Hill in Kansas

for John Dorsey

i remember it here & there
drinking those dark mysteries
like children at water balloon play
who scored smiles from underneath
those pimp-hats of   oblivion

i felt it like a string of Christmas lights
with their rapid succession of changing moods

until
the great composer
cried with only one hand over his face
because the other one
was too busy strangling
the hearts of the weak

& we drank Christ off the cross
        until Revelations made sense

until our throats
        our veins
        our blood

began to feel like an empty house
with a lost bird inside

banging against the glass
of eternally locked windows

Stealing Home

i remember aunt Barbara,
58 years old & 110 pounds,
sitting on the porch, drinking gin
& watching us play baseball

she'd stagger off the porch,
with long & stringy pepper-colored hair
that flapped around her ears,
and she'd pull up the elastic band of her pants,
push me out of the way,
& grab the bat

Barbara, swiveling her hips, settling in
just like Jim Rice,
she would tap the head of the bat
& spit on the milk carton
we used as home plate

when the pitch came in,
Barbara eased in & let it fly,
right over third base & completely
out of reach

she ran the bases like a prize winning horse,
slamming her foot on each one
until she jumped in the air
& slammed both feet on third

a few months later,
i remember my aunt Barbara
in her coffin

they took her booze away,
so she began to drink the cleaning products
from under the sink

always good at reading those signals,
she'd steal home with ease.

Brother Kancamagus

i shut my eyes
        in an armchair of Swift River
wavering between the quiets
   & the ruckus inside man
estranged for what i thought i've known
     i notice
what is actually beating
          is the song of my cadaver
& i pull from Rocky Gorge
                  & autumn tribe
(ruled by war chiefs)
     to see the fears of my life
          & i notice
the years that have been missed
     like a November sun
                  staining my face
that sleeps with me   –awake
     in the partial sounds of space
& this thought
     to be set free
in a passing moment of wind
          watches the hawk fly away
onto a road of pine trees
   & mountain lines
               vanishing
conspiring
        its escape.

The Slow Side of the Street

i try to think of any dream
of myself walking
the slower sides of the street
—always
with a head full of shit.

i bend over,
feeling the fat drink itself
inside the cold sky
within the hateful immensity
of those that call things
forever or eternal,

and realize the truth has been fucked
—over and over
in the back end
of an old black and white French film,
wind still blowing, cold
truth cries rape,
dripping a torture of humanity
from its knife slits
—falling
onto the prison of its knees,
but
freedom never comes,
not from birth,
not from death.

The tomb of this universe
is a slow dying love
in every face i see,
walking
the slow streets
within me.

Hiking the Mind of God

to be banished beyond memory & thought,
you set out as the flow of a rumbling snow-blind.
                    Expanding
 with the rage of jutting-rocks, piercing vast & wide open
distances,
& the silence is but its own mirror, the true self, forever boundless,

climbing dome of sky.
                    Unsettling,
into atmospheric seascapes of endless nowhere
grip rock nooks
                    of limitless white powdered pools
that bathe in the stretching valleys of your continuous palace.

                    No end in sight.

Thoughts grow countless within the greatness of the mist,
        a cocoon   of   snowdrift   to   separate
                    many pieces of self
                            into one.

        Wandering around...

Quietly
reaching
through
the
self,

standing (alone)
finally.
                    Discovering home.

Unsheathed

it said
coming home would be blinded
by betrayal & its great place in denial
from a distance beyond conception,
the modest companion is seldom wanted
when the shadowy limbs teethe with identification.

and man, like the blind mouth, still lives
to endure violence
in the beauty of his mind,
with a chaos of thirst pouring from his hands,
like a violin that moves slowly in bleeding velvets.

it warned
not of a fear of death,
but a fear of relaxed arrogance,
unsheathed by the human incapacity to dream,
like empty footed stallions drinking moonlight
in praise of their split tragedies to strengthen the miracles
& mock the timeless civilizations of foresight.

and the sky buried torment in delusions of grandeur,
as clay pots of flesh pulled whirlwinds of passion
out of soft-feminine-feathers.

without any talons it waited for death
like a reflected desire that is self-woven
on top of the heads of holy birds
who answer to the prophets without love,

who point out their great labors
with beautiful flames,
that dance in desire & power
in the age of renewal.

it became the death of blasphemy,
and it said,
this is nevertheless
the agony of ourselves.

Nowhere Town

when the gin hit
i was staggering down the boardwalk
& stepping on the carnival lights

i shuffled between the people
who laughed & hugged a lot

they carried giant stuffed animals under their arms
they sucked down extra-large colas
& devoured colorful cotton candy

& when the moonlight finally closed for business
i sat on the beach & opened a candy bar

i dropped the wrapper & watched it blow into the waves
& when i fell into the sand & looked up into the stars
my thoughts were mixed into the poisons of loneliness

that dome of twinkling lights sitting above my face
it meets at the far points of the ocean
& it touches upon the dreams of people i've never met
& yet somehow we are all here together
on this same lonely avenue
roaring back & forth

a bunch of wrappers
blowing somehow
outta nowhere town.

Her Rites

for Erin Reardon

it was the darkness that caught her up as
she swallowed
tiny white anniversaries
that bore her a doom child
named of her own death

and those men of difficult need
took hours
from her levitating-silk-coated heart

she thought of them as wild boys
who rolled around in her belly
as cement mixers
on clean white sheets
(they moved as Roman sexualities)

her body–
a holiday among gods
was laced in pink clouded moonlight
love and she
played with invisible faces
to choose whom to find natural beauty with

in her hands
(that greased straight lines
on the skins of their beds)
she found the delicate foam of hours waiting
to be touched by the violet skies
that kissed her hair

knowing after-shock
she let nicotine rings wrap the head
for she did not want to stay long

not in want nor lust
not in element nor in feeling

and the child that was her pain
locked her up inside secret wars
one day to rise as a rose but roses

62

upon birth slowly die
alive & gorgeous
then wilted & framed madness

and she fell to the ground
sleeping but not gone
shaking
with a dark arrow
lodged deeply into the sorrow
of the 100 country songs
that kicked inside her blood

and with a slow & tender mercy
from her dry lips
and a conversation
within the lonely places
of crowded gestures

the envy for her life
became forever seized
in the rites
of her holy sacrifice.

3 Quarters for Ol' Blind Chester

For years
Ol' blind Chester
picked his guitar
in front of The Corner Mall
in Downtown Crossing

He played from the morning light
all the way to that moonlight turn around,
sitting on the same milk crate
with the same guitar case open,
collecting nickels, dimes, & even dollar bills

They took my eyes when i was boy, he'd say,
sliding that clear bone along the strings of his steel guitar,

But i don't wanna take their eyes, oh no, not ever,
his fingers picking those same open chords

Because they'd never be able to see what i feel,
oh no, never be able to see what i feel,
and son, what is the use in a whole world
not being able to see?
Because you gots to have the guts to look at me,
if you truly wanna be set free...

Rucksack Hungry

& the highway said:

the desire
inside
the   loner
is
an
ember

learning
            to burn

its
way

through

the

asylum,

Fuck
You
& your
suicide,

Hart Crane.

Answering Your Own Questions

when she took off her tight vinyl pants
& crawled into my bed,
she said, "i have no idea what a poem is
or what one does."

i said nothing
while my hands parted her legs
& my tongue jumped into her small bed of curls

it was only a matter of time
until she figured it out
on her
own.

The Loneliness of a Bed

right after we fucked
she lit two cigarettes
in the darkness of her lips
& handed me one

"seeing the
world for what it is
really hurts." she said

i said nothing
letting the tip of my
cigarette
become the light for
the both of us

i was just too
tired to
die.

The Big Papa Blues

The only
natural
thing
that Ernie
could do

was to jam
both barrels
into his kisser

& pull the
trigger

at last,

all of
his
words
could
finally
breathe.

The People

the words are
becoming
the people
that i
like to be
around
but don't
want to
speak to.

The Grim Reaper in Lotus

the grim reaper
sat in lotus
& picked flowers
as i cracked
the spine
of yet
another writer
who used
big words
& distant
language.
as he ripped
more from
the ground,
i looked
over at the
visceral
colors of
the flowers
that he had
in his hands,
& he said to me,
"it's okay,
they've been
fooled before
too,
just know,
there is
no such thing
as a legacy,
only death."

Nearly Making It

And buy "hope"
a drink
too,

it's my
last five, but

he looks
like he
needs
it more
than I
do.

Snowflake Beautiful

Erin,
you & i
had to pretend
that 3 leaf clovers were 4.

We had to shoot pistols without bullets,
turn knobs without doors,
& drink beer without the bottle.

Our names were prison & orphan,
and we were trapped
in the despair of folklore
while we crunched up stars
& snorted them off the ass
of Wyoma Square.

We'd count dollars
as if they were lost children,
& with a ball & chain strut,
we'd hit The Four Winds
like a couple of kings
that had just lost their crowns.

We would pour our love making faces
onto the bar of the unwanted.

Our bellies were like lips
that sucked up the vitamins from the rails,
& we'd speak to each other only to forget.

We sat close to blind memory,
drinking the bone yard out of heaven
with our eyes fixated
on the 7th inning stretch.

It never mattered if they won or lost,
because either way
the worms would still be moving
on their fast track to our deaths.

We'd be snowflake beautiful
when leaving like a crowd of clouds

72

trying to find the sky,

You, singing a Lucinda Williams song
to the 4 pm work traffic,
and me, throwing up
on the sides of the buildings.

We'd go across the street to the packie,
grab four 40 ounces of King Cobra,
& stagger back to your mother's house
mumbling through the lonely sounds
of cars cutting through the wind.

Never saying a word,
we'd be as silent as the twilight of the void,
eating stewed tomatoes & pasta
and sipping warm tap water.

After opening those 40 ounces
with our half smiles of the defeated,
we'd laugh for no reason,
the sleepy sounds
of Joe Castiglione
on the radio.

Earning Respect

After all those years
of taking beatings
from my father,
i was ready
to earn his respect
by finally hitting back, but
gaining a father's respect
takes a lot
of direct hits.

It is a lot like a poem
in a certain respect,
because after knocking
your father down
for the first time,
you've got to be able
to know how to take
the beating & bruising
that he is going
to inflict on you
when he finally stands
back up.

Burnt Girl

She showed me a picture of herself from 1981.
Her hair was long & brown,
and i thought to myself
that she could have been a ballerina
or a model in Paris or Berlin.

Now she was in her 40's,
& her face looked burned from some fire,
but i did not ask why.
i just watched the rain wash into the gutters.
It reflected into the bar mirror in front of me
from the window behind me.

Looking over at me, she said, *life does strange things to you,*
& when you finally realize it, it's too late to know
what you could have done with it.

i felt bad, so i invited her to a party, ordered her a drink,
& played more Rolling Stones on the juke box.
i started to smell her scent from her picture,
& it blasted my brains out the back of my head
& onto the window behind me,
where the rain was running into the gutters.

When i finally stopped looking through
the two way reflections,
there was a fat black man standing next to her.
He called her a *bitch,*
& he looked like he was waiting for a response out of her.

But she just sat there, said nothing,
& began to cry into the drink i had just bought her.
It must have been because of all the rain.

Sometimes
we just forget
to let all our animals in.

Then You Got the Blues

when you tried
to hustle
pain
by drinking,
pain
had already
rolled the dice &
hustled your
shadows,
leaving
you
on the side of
the road,
stripped down
to the core,
with no place
to go,
with nothing more
than a choice
between
100 different
sins,
with nothing
more than
your last
bone
& moan.

The Little Boy

The little boy inside
of me is scared.

He tells me
that it is dark in here
& that he needs to
come out, hug me,
& call me daddy.

He throws punches
at the lining
of my
soul, so i'll
listen to
him cry.

He furiously
kicks the walls of
my heart,
so i won't forget
his face
& the reasons
why he is
still alive.

He stands alone
in the darkness
& ulcers of
my stomach,

a blonde hair
little boy who asks
why? over &
over.

He puts his head down
when he feels
he has done something
wrong.

He fidgets & rubs
his hands

& fingers together
when i stop
paying attention
to him.

He swallows
the key to
my thoughts
when i
try to drink
him away.

He makes big
fists with
his tiny hands
when i take
anti-hypochondria
medication.

He skips rope
with my intestines
when i write
poems.

The little boy inside
does not know
that i am
on the wrong side
of 30.

He knows
nothing
about the
white in my beard.

He just wants
out of the wild &
lonely frontier
that he has been
trapped in

& he wants
to come out,
touch my

face, & let
me know that
the longer i deny
him, the longer

he will let me
keep believing
that love
will never be
enough.

A Letter to Lowell

Lowell,
how did i get here?
i
cannot
escape   what
                i am.

face
in mirror
        is still the same, different,
weathered many storms, Lowell,
the blood
of spine, creased,
        creature-d, & insisting on mysticism.

the road, a graduation,
& i seem to be happy about the direction
            the nails   were   hammered,
but the human inside
wants to shed
the pain   & escape.

But I cannot escape
what I am,
can I, Lowell?

Too many generations of flowers
                have bloomed
                    & withered,
& I stand here,
10,000 miles later,
            stove-d in by the past,
trying to
& trying to,

but the black ghost inside
keeps avoiding the sermon of the eyes,
(he is as black as tornado juice, dripping
on entities that know nothing of secrets.)

Black ghost keeps silent screams.
Black ghost keeps tribe away from the nude.

Black ghost knows to stay & keep thirsty.

Lowell,
        his own is my own,
        a child without protection
        in a man's world of lost thunder.

& the photographs
        of boy, 25 years earlier,
        is a different life, unknown to
        the present actions of activity,
        immersed in salted baptisms,
        & he cries, locked in dungeon

    not released & not escaping, Lowell.

The black ghost
                has not called for the death of the poet yet,
so
how
will i
know
when
i
can
unlock

& free the wise-man?

How
will
i
know, Lowell,

when love will be the all
& i can let go?

Lowell, two men at the bar
            said to me, *you've been around,*
like an aging mountain of unknown artwork.
Are my hands shaking that bad?
Is my face without clown makeup?

Can i

break my jaw
& open my mouth
                (with both hands,
letting the long
& dark roads
scream from my belly, moving,
as fast
as the truck driver
strung out
on weeks
of early morning
diner amphetamine?)

Lowell, the crowds are amassing.
They say nothing,
believe in nothing,
                look at nothing,
                echo nothing,

  & it seems as if the battle has been wasted
     on the tiny left over particles of sociopath,
  or delivered
     into narrow roots of transmitters.
     Soft is hard   waiting

on the light from third eye wilderness,
          but the songs are too strange, Lowell,

& the house is without self,
                occupied by others,
(priest
drunk
father
writer
mountaineer
slouch
child
doctor.)
             They consume everything,
             refuse anything,

& they listen to the black ghost give them orders;
how to be
& how to act.

I need that key, Lowell,
I need to unlock the house & purify it,
write outside the lines,
       & batter, to pulp & song,
       the desires of Oedipus Rex.

As space continuum
to where
to be, similar & in need,

breathing its new life,
       no boundary,
       no time,

only passion,
observer,

silence

Gardens Grow All Kinds of Things

After my
grandfather
got home
from
fucking the
woman
with one good
eye,

& after he
ate a steak
bigger than
ours,

& after he
slapped
around my
grandmother
a little bit,

& after
he went into
the liquor
cabinet,

he'd go into
his garden
& start to
unwind.

i'd sit in his
garden
with him

and watch his
big hands pull
at weeds
& throw stones
over his
shoulders.

To him, nothing was

ever in its
right place.

Everything
was always
out of
place,

except for that
bottle of
rum

sitting next
to his hip,
sugary
& glowing
in the sun,

waiting
for him
to grab it
by its neck
& tilt it
upside down.

& after all the
grumbling,
cursing,
& all of the middle
fingers that
he gave
to things that
would not
grow,

it was nice
to finally
see him
calm down.

Promise Me That Grave Site

& let me vanish
into the
rain & thunder.

it is the only
prison
that has
ever listened.

The Hot Poker

Patti
would play
20th Century Boy
by T Rex

when she
wanted it.

Stripping
down to nothing
but her old
beat up
doc martens,
she'd bend
over my
bureau

& shake her
chunky ass
back &
forth.

She'd say,
"Get over here, Reardon,
& give me that
hot poker of yours."

It was the
first time
i ever understood
art.

All Those Dying Daisies
on All Those Mantles of the World

every single
cigarette
that i crushed
into those lonely
yellow glass
hotel ashtrays
of the world,

& every single
beer that i
guzzled,
smashed,
& tossed

while making
a last minute
buzzer sound,

was a love poem
to you.

I Don't Care How You Write

if the gods
are not doubled over
& clenching their guts
from the "jabs" you
just threw at your
typewriter, then
it's not
a poem.

Tobin Bridge

It was always like that,
riding over you, Tobin Bridge,
from Ol' ragged Chelsea
with its half sheets
of dead-eyed workers,
with its old time men
on stools headed hell-bound,
with its 3-4 storied homes
where families looked out
from windows decorated
in rosary beads
and catholic wishes.

O' your peeling rust
of green stained steel rails,
how you captured their faces
like strings
of unsuccessful novels,
and it seemed like it took forever
to drive over you,
underneath your upper deck,
with large iron beams
and eye holes of forever,
with thumps of cars above,
who were on their way
to the North Shore
for picnics full of hot dog
and mustard story time
while sitting in postage stamp
sized backyards.

And i can see,
on the other side of you,
parades of dashing
yellow city lights,
people jumbling around,
shops and street cart vendors
yelling in different languages,
and in the distance,
sitting like a guardian,
a tall building with a giant clock
on top, the one i used to tell

90

my grandfather was Big Ben,
the keeper, the old wise monk,
always watching over Boston,
proud, filthy and marvelous Boston,
waiting for us on the other side
next to the trash scented Mystic,
hugged by the cold Atlantic,
and we'd thump
on explosive street bumps,
with endless cars
speeding to this way
and that way,
honking with prayers and laughter,
and with each second
that enormous Boston got closer
with its aching beauty.

The paralyzed steam songs
from smoke stacks
of Everett's candy mill
would vanish from my eyes,
cranes touching the sky
from docks of Southie
would lose touch,
distant beaches
filled with Italian tough guys
from far off Revere
would become a thing of the past,
but once i saw
that giant shamrock
on the brick face
of the Garden,
where endless 3 pointers
were scored,
where endless hat tricks
made broke fathers
throw ball caps onto the ice,
where singers, of all kinds,
from all sorts of places
like Cleveland, Atlanta
and Paris would come to sing,
as soon as i saw you,
brick faced protector
of North Station,

i knew that my ride
over old green Tobin was over.

i knew that the 50 cents
paid to indifferent toll man
had been used up,
i knew that i was now
in the place of those
who came before me,
where millions of hard footed
business men
with expensive suits
and long heavy faces
would rush to Haymarket buses,
where cabs honked
and police whistles
blasted into the night
next to rows and rows
of torn out concrete,
where construction workers
with tank tops
jack hammered
streets corners
while shouting
at ladies in short skirts
and numerous shades
of lipstick.

It was those feelings,
those scents
and senses of belief,
and harmony
that was given to us by you,
long and lonely Tobin,
with your fog horns
and images of long ago,
it's wise the way you sit above us,
waiting like the toiled upon
years of a desert snake
who had shed
too many skins,
it's your passion
that came from early century
steelworkers,

who ached agony
into your backbone
on platforms built
out of necessity,
who painted you the color
of excited ancestors
who rushed over on tons
of boats, it's you, Tobin,
who watches us all,
protects us all,
it's you that stands
like the barrel chested warrior
above the streets
of unsuspected living,
it's you who is waiting,
watching,
grieving,
and no one would have ever
been the wiser
to have even noticed
just how long you've
actually been
listening.

B-57

for RAZOR

It was windy in Los Angeles
when Frank O'Hara delivered a letter,
"*Love is not a Goodbye,*"
and in deliverance, with hand strangling coffee cup
of mad-electric hair, the last breath from a raven
now listened.
In his B-57, painted in gold coast dreams,
he laughed tears before bars
with the tiny mechanical parts that flew away.
Far past Malibu Pass
as a sky pilot, hovering above the ravines,
he crashed into the brain of his words,
and I watched him try to navigate the stratosphere
in exploding pieces of   *near to her*
                                                                  and *away from her.*

 He knew all too well
that white clouds
          have also *struggled*
                    to find their way   into heaven.

Postcards From Chinatown

Maybe
the
moon
knows
me all
too well,
because
i can
feel
its "love"
cutting
through
my nerves
with
the howlin'
agony
of alley
cats,
& i
can
hear
its voice
in the
doomed
whistling
of
trash
men
who
break
lonely
3 a.m.
bottles
on the
side
of the
road.

Drop the Stockings of Any Symphony

if you want to own
everything
& everyone
in a room,

unsnap the garters
of a symphony,
drop its stockings,
pick your instrument,
& play the tune.

The Mortal Kids

michael lived
around the corner
from me
when he hung
himself.

it was said
that his girlfriend
dumped him,
so he went
into his
basement,
grabbed
a rope & bucket,
& jumped.

people said
his mother found him,
& she dropped
the 12 piece
bucket of chicken
she had bought
for dinner
by his feet.

she grabbed
his legs
& tried to push
him up,
trying to save his
already dead life.

they said
his fingers were broken
because when he dropped
he had changed
his mind,
putting his fingers
into the rope,
each one
snapping like
a twig

from the weight
of his swinging
body.

a lot of people
were at the funeral.
teachers who
did not teach him
& did not
know him
had a lot to say
about him,
girls & boys
who hated him
were holding
one another
& crying.

shannon & i
sat in the back
of Saint Teresa's.
we did not say much
or do much.
we really did
not know him.

we got up & left
half way through
the funeral,
& we cut through
the woods in our
funeral clothes,
saying nothing
to one another.

& when we arrived
at shannon's house,
we took our clothes off
& lost our virginity.

no words were ever said
between us
as we both sat there, naked.

feeling like a couple
of mortals
for the first time
was more
than enough.

Locating Marvelous Marvin Hagler

at six years old,
i was near death
with pneumonia,

& to remove the mucus,
the doctors would hang me
upside down & slap my back
over & over until i cried.

their red hand prints
decorated my skin.

i could see
in their faces
that their efforts
were failing.

my teachers
came to visit me,
my aunt
filled my bed
with soldiers,
 cards were
sent to me,
& my room
had become
a florist sale.

my grandfather
started coming
to see me
every afternoon.

he'd stink of cigars
& rum.

he'd read me
articles of boxing matches,
explaining every detail
of how Marvelous Marvin
would look defeated
& down for the count,

how his body was wrecked,
eyes pulped,
& jaw smashed,
but Marvin got up
& won in the tenth.

his opponent had
underestimated
his will to survive.

my grandfather's voice
sounded like
a ring side announcer
as he read me
the blow by blow accounts,
& my heart would pump
faster & faster.

my lungs sucked air
like a horse
on the last stretch,

& the doctors sat stumped
with all their training
& medical knowledge.

they had no idea
or understanding
why they could not
locate my spirit
& give me the will
to survive.

Saint Francis of New England

When the momentum changes, the emotions
take over,
            & luck is on its knees, grievous
                    & left alone, exposed,

or
a rolling ocean
that can conquer the last of the lonely kids
in rowboats without paddles,

but to make sure of infinity,
cut the heart out & use it as an umbrella, protecting
the long road of winded body song from the storm.

In evening's house of death,
you can see the disguise
sounding otherwise

as, in the life of sketched missiles, in adored lust:

the saloon of memory, later, much longer
in opened mouths of slipped velvet tongues
                    in sequences of touch,

but
feeling was differently heard:
(in animal sounds
on hollow vein-y paths–

            pulsing contrary objects of tissue
            in complexity's reflection of birth.

Passion of flesh machine,
possibility to admire, find & fault,
answering the mind of peeling rock,
leaving embracing blood in the music of love,

            emotion is, as changing bird
            colors
            of birth
            & states in between events
            of origin,

102

presented with self
to see involvement.
What is done
& appears
in tiny messages
of random pains, admired
by flowers, rising
with involvement

moment to moment,
in the petals that have fallen to the floor.
Justice is no longer involved
with the appetites for skin
& from the dirtiness within

whence it flowed,
to arise,
to transcend,
to trample soul,
to unravel silence,
to defend,
to hold & pry,
to protect sound,
to develop & contemplate,
to play the part,
to enter,
to be who as blood talks through,
to stiffen,
to pluck the rose,
to smell, to devour,
to taste, to imagine.

Momentum!
Hallelujah!
Hallelujah!
Hallelujah!

The great benevolence of the gesture, in awe,
in supreme closeness to holy,

bearing you, O great razor of the sun,
kiss me with great circumstance
for I have cheated your death,
& it is i who am alive!

103

Scraping Chairs

The gunshot went off
as i lost my last pinball.

The chair legs scraped
across the floor
followed by a large thud.
something had collapsed.

Turning the corner,
i shook in curiosity & fear.
There was a man lying
on the floor,
a face i had never seen,
a face i had never cared about.

He spewed a purple river
from his mouth,
his insides leaking over his
left hand as he held his chest.

His legs kicked and locked,
the feet separated from their
90 degree angle.
He looked over at me
(lips coated in a purple/red)
brown eyes faded and shut.

Uncle Jimmy & Cousin Stan
covered him in a canvas tarp
moving fast, picking him up,
moving him toward the backdoor.

They never took notice of me.
Piss had run down
my 8-year-old legs,
staining my brown cords.

After they had put him in the van,
Uncle Jimmy did a bump off his hand.

Reaching into his pocket,
he pulled out a bunch of change.

Putting it into my tiny hands,
he told me to play pinball.
He told me he'd be back real soon.
He told me the guys here would watch me.

That night
when i was trying to sleep,
someone pulled the chair
across the floor.

i wet the bed
for the next 6 years.

Boston Irish

These people, my people,
have always been called the quiet ones,
stuck in a manifested silence,
spoken with a nod, a punch, or from the ale glass.

Living by hand and a scar's promise,
they guide paranoid notions
with the promise of patience.
In the quiet of their suffering
is the strength of their song,
while they count on the prayers
and the luck from a silver saint's medal.

Bodies bruised by unconscious words,
drunk in the spits of victory,
they claim all spirits to be safe,
and with arms locked inside one another,
they serenade the night,
voices in parade down Huntington and Yawkey,
but in the deep eternal well of silence
they forget how to weep.

These people, my people,
the rovers of ancient things that are calmed in solitude,
find peace in recovering from injuries,
placing large ice packs onto wrenched bodies
while still finding time to make bird calls to empty ceilings.

Hard-over-worked-blue-collar-symphonies
trapped in the blink of an eye that could tell a story of panic,
gaze wildly upon bar rooms,
looking for the flame,
trying to keep the mistress from marrying the rage.

Arched Ceilings

Ginny & i
had an attic apartment
on Day St. in Jamaica Plain.
Our bathroom ceilings came down in an arch.
We could not stand up to take showers.
We'd always had to take baths.

She'd sit & soak,
the tips of her red hair dancing in the water,
washcloth over her eyes,
& 90's grunge playing throughout the apartment.

i'd peek through the crack of the door,
her large breasts covered by the soapy water,
frustration flowing throughout the tub
from her skin,
from places she could not cry from.

She tried hard to dance her smiles.
She tried hard to pull her hands from hell
& place them into heaven,
but all she knew how to do was arch her head to the right
& take it all in.

i was always too busy snorting up our savings account
to even notice that what she really needed
was to be able to stand up straight
& wash off all the things that i had done wrong.

Extremes

"i hate the universe
& everything
in it, it's time
to make
some serious
changes"
a man
shouted through
clenched
teeth, as he
read
the news
headlines.

"i love the magic
of the universe
& everything
in it." a woman
wearing Teva's
said, while
breast feeding,
&reading a book
of Gandhi
quotes.

"i can see the universe
for what it is."
said an old man
as he took
random
snap shots
of the flowers
in the park
garden.

& when the old man
looked
at the pictures
on his camera,
he noticed
that some
of the flowers

were dying,
while others
were alive with
color & beauty.

upon noticing
the two
extremes,
he immediately
stopped
looking
at the pictures,
leaned back,
& violently
began
to laugh.

Muse Dogs (for Venice Beach)

Never having been to Venice,
i'll make an excuse for my blood
& write its cracked sunshine,
giving myself a past through
the eyes of my heart's imagination.

In your graffiti of humanity,
everyone dies at some time
with their living ghosts, jaded
        in the taking
from your palm tree love songs,
from your sandy-footed past time.

In your worded wings as wind
            of Scibella
            of Perkoff

as mechanical devices,
            danger languages
created out of rag dolls sleeping
            stronger before
                    lonely,
    a mountain top
            in the face
                of the pacific.
Rising orchestra of muse dogs
plunging knife
into sounds of sunset gods,
    listening through ears
    of ongoing tragedies.

As hush points of the fingertip
    touching
the atmospheric
                unseen,
caress
is
found.

Never having made love to Venice,
    i purchased plane tickets
so i could

                  scream as a hungry hawk
within her blood tubes,
  to dance a massive piece energy
                  EXPLODING
      all inside her skirt,
that i am about
                  to lift
with the curiosity
of
a
baby blue,
                  sweetly.

An Alabama Baptism

If you're down on your luck then Jesus has a cold one inside.

Of course i
am a bit shy, What else?
Driving through the red lights of my mind,
staggering, straight inside. Commanding.

Plush purple velvet carpets,
the smell of fresh hands
& clean organs that pumped persuasion,
no matter where i looked,
i seem to be here, harmonized.

Preacher at the pulpit with
arms opened,
pearly whites for the money,
& a prominence for Revelation's recurrence.

i had thoughts for Saint John.
i added a picture as well.
i was trying to proclaim communication
about the darkness that surrounds us,

but what i found out
was that i addressed the thought to myself,
"Good Lord, was i late."

Tons of hands on my head,
tongues flipping flows of after-sight,
& my robe, my white-white robe, soaked
in the fibers of my busted stitches.

Perpetually weeping
by the *Lord's* side, i wanted it
like it was before.

Time Bomb

there is this certain sadness
in the stillness of your voice
that only the piled up dirty
dishes in your sink
& all the large rings of smoke
from your 17th butt in a row
could ever understand.

They're Saying Something in Italian
& It Makes Me Weep

the only *revolution*
i need
is to fall
onto my couch
& *occupy* its
broken springs
while Beatrice di Tenda
sinks me into tears
& wails me to sleep.

They Are Speaking In Meat Cleaver

don't forget
to build
a trench
& sharpen
your
bayonet
while
visiting other
people's
minds.
they are
stringing up
beef in
there
& their
songs have
already
riled up
the armies
of the world.

His Red Hand

i took great pride
in being able
to drink anyone i knew
under the table

i would stagger
out of the pubs
as if i was a
great champion
with class & style

it was an art form
like busting balls,
stealing a car,
or landing
the first punch
in a barroom brawl

& now, after
10 generations of flowers
have come & gone,
i feel brother death
hanging over my shoulder
& laughing

he has given me
the great hitch
that is now in my step,
with a glassy set of eyes,
fat-swollen knuckles
& a mouth that won't quit

& when i approach
any crosswalk outside
of any pub in the world,
there are no longer
anymore crossing buttons
for me to press

those white lines
on the pavement
that were a bridge

to carry me
to the other side
have narrowed

 it has left me
with nothing more
than his red hand
& it keeps blinking

over
& over –

Stop!

All the Lonely Screams
from All the Lonely Dirt Road Dogs

i feel sorry for all of the dirt roads
& filthy back alleyways of the world.

While everyone has been busy
riding their superhighways
& intellectual interstates to nowhere,

the salivating, hungry, & barking dogs,
ready to rip you apart
from the other side of their fences,
have been put out of business.

A Year on the Couch

I have not seen you in so long,
where have you been? she asked.

i don't know,
i woke up on the couch,
i think i have been on the couch for an entire year.

An entire year!
How did you manage that?

The last thing i can remember...

i went out for a walk,
everything was beautiful,
the sun was out,
the flowers were dancing for me,
the birds were singing,

& i remember shouting to myself,
Finally!

Then
i came home
& i had to sit down...

For Scott Wannberg

Maybe
death
is such
a hard
thing
to write
about

because
there
is no
death
when
a giant
falls,

there
is only
this
imprint
left in
the soil
of our
heart,

& it leaves
an eternal
mark,
waiting
for us
to touch,
see,
feel,
& recognize.

Visions of Being Human

poetry –
what else should it be
besides the Harley Davidson
shining under the moon
of a 2 a.m. bar,

the sexy woman who
slowly straddles
the back of the bike
with her tight jeans
& foul language,

the revving of the engine
versus the back door of the bar
that slowly closes
onto that last piece of wind,

like a violent pop of pulp
that traps Steve Marriott's
screaming voice
back into the bar
& forever sealing it
within the tiniest cracks
of your whiskey-soaked soul.

The Know-It-All

The barefooted woman, wearing her designer clothes,
took to the stage to read her poems.

"Namaste everyone! My name is Morgan!"
she emphatically shouted.

She kicked around in her bare feet,
that were rubbed in expensive oils,
& she proudly wore a Mitt Romney T-shirt,
the kind with a giant red X over Mitt's face.

"I have a poem I made out of one of my VEGAN recipes!"

She went on & on about tofu
& bean pods.

"My next poem is about SQUIRREL SAFETY!"

While she read her fantasy poem
about humans getting jobs as squirrel crossing guards,
i watched her hips in her tight designer corduroys,
& i wondered why she wore a scarf in 90 degree weather.
It was the color of the rainbow, & it tickled her hips.
i imagined that scarf being my hands.

"My next poem is about MEAN MR. OIL!"

The people stood up & applauded,
then they went stark raving mad, they foamed at the mouth,
men cried, women turned lesbian on the spot.

They shouted & hissed every time she said *"gas prices."*
They leaped up & ran the walls like angry caged monkeys
when she yelled, *"Support our troops & get them out of there!"*

She had them all at attention.
These people had waited all of their lives to be led,
& Morgan was there for them,
ready & willing to take them out of bondage.

"Do I have time for one more poem?"

They cheered, hooted, & hollered,
they demanded more,
the guy running the event nodded yes.

"Okay! This is my poem about the need for love!"

But Morgan had a trick for this poem.
Not only was it a poem about the universe, love, & caring,
but it was a rap poem, & she even included a little dance.

That was all the people needed to see & hear.
They walked to the back of the room,
preformed Inquisitions.
They began to kick over tables, tie people to poles,
& set them on fire.

The more & more she rapped about love,
the more they killed, raped, beat, maimed, & murdered.

The more & more she said
we all must follow our heart's calling,
the more tables, chairs, & children
went flying through windows.

The biggest bitch of it all,
my beer instantly turned
into grapefruit juice.

All Roads Lead to the Ranger Bar

When the drunk Indian at The Ranger bar
called me *Bullshit*
i realized i was never going to make it as a writer.

i took it out on the universe.
i shouted at April.
All my hard livin',
all my hard work,
went out the door with lunatics!

i told her,
"Not even the bikers looked at me with respect.
The Sargent of Arms stared at me. He waited for me
to make a move, but i walked out the door. i was
a coward."

She rolled her eyes, said nothing, & went back to her beer.

Standing over the toilet,
with my cock in hand,
i swerved my body back & forth.

"Fucking goddamn Indian," i mumbled to myself.
i had grown forever tired of living in the country.
Maybe it has been good for me, i dunno.

One thing was for certain,
while i was pissing, it got all over my pants,
the toilet seat,
& the floor,
"Fuckin' Goddamn Indian!"

i had been hitting everything but the center.

Boney Finger

Conduct your body of agony
to the screams in Beethoven's 9th

drenching all those fields
in the valley of the lost

& by the madness of your tears
you'll soon see the skeletons
growing within the flowers

True Test

if you want to know
if you've still
got it, the fire,
all you
have to do
is step outside
& watch how
all the beautiful
asses of all
the beautiful women
move around
before your eyes

but

if it has left you,
you'll begin to suffer
over bills,
you'll go shopping
& buy too many things,
you'll go to an
emergency room
for no reason
at all, &
you'll start
to call yourself
a poet, & give
yourself a name
like *The Poet Earthen Claw*

but

if it's there,
you'll know it,
you'll dance
with the flowers,
you'll write a song,
you'll write
a poem, you'll
laugh while
you are all alone,
you'll drag death

126

around the barn
& put two into
his head,
you'll look up
at the stars &
trace out pictures
with your finger,
you'll open
a can of beer
just so you can
hear the snap
& fizzle sound
that it makes,
you'll take off your shirt,
& pants,
& sit on the floor
of your living room,
for no reason
at all, other than,
the feeling
of your bare flesh
resting
on the rug,

don't try & find it
in books, or
in philosophical
debates, don't look
for it in politics,
or in online chat rooms,
don't seek it
in religion, or
in a god,
you won't find
it in those places,

don't be like those people,
those that fear simplicity,

don't lie to get it,
or kill to get it,
it's not really
that complicated.

The Big Sky

No one has been on this hill in ages,
with its dirt path heading downwards
& park bench without a seat

where Bill carved
that he loved Alice
inside a jagged heart.

i stand so far away from everything
that i have become a part of its ritual.

Big sky
    (bursting)
        enormous country.

i am alone,
alone as it is to be human,
alone as the carving on this broken bench

& with any luck,
the living will let me stay here a little longer.

Breaking Through Oak

Grandpa stood on the edge of the lawn,
looking up at the large oak in our backyard.

Still in his greasy work shirt, Dickies,
& broken leather shoes,
he had one beer by his side, tucked neatly into his hand,
slightly ready to fall from the day's sweat.

He looked older than the week before,
his blue eyes squinting from behind his glasses,
his face had grown agony's tired stubble,
& he would not motion nor speak to me.

The hair tonic had lost its power over his gray hair,
moving it around in small fights with the wind,
while he stood there letting his cigar smoke
take over the lines of his face.

i looked up with him,
i tried to imitate him, but
he did not take any notice of me.

He just kept gazing at the oak's branches
& how small pieces of the dusk's sun tried to break through
the darkest areas of the branches.

"Grandpa, what do you see?" i asked him.
"Shhhh..." he said, "don't you see it?"
"See what, Grandpa?"
"Everything is finally quiet."

They Prepare Too Much

when you tape up
your knuckles,
you only
give the words
a chance
to escape you.

Perryton, Texas

Humanity first appeared
to me at 8 years old,

sitting in a chair outside
my father's hotel room
in Perryton, Texas.

i was using my first
pocket knife,

carving away, violently,
at a piece of wood
that i had found
on the ground.

i looked to the left of me,
silence & oaks,
to my right,
a Mexican woman
cleaning a hotel room

& down on my lap,
i noticed that i had
sliced open my hand,
& strangely enough
it did not hurt.

This new puddle of blood,
red & isolated
by my flesh,
fell in love with exile.

It Isn't the First Time
I've Been Called Howard Hughes

"If your writing is so real,
then what is with all these
fist fights, temper tantrums,
& screams of hunger?"

i lit a cigarette,
forcefully blew out
the first drag with a sigh,
pointed to the ground,
& said,

"Do you see that bluejay
& how it's struggling
to devour that worm?"

10 Years

if i could explain
10 years
any better to you,
i would,
but the rubber
to the road
gave the fingers
a notion
of the heart
that pounds the typing
machine
& holds the bottle.

10 years
never had anything
profound to say,
it never understood
how to say goodbye
properly,
or how to age
with birthdays,
its soul had always
been
found
in the silence
of every moving bus
window
of every town
that it had
already left.

10 years
was the Christmas card
mailed
without a reply,
it was every
religious sentiment
seen on a big sign
outside Greenville
& Fort Worth,
while the mouth
chomped on

another fried meal
that had been
wrapped up
by three days
ago.

10 years
turned
the loving man
into the cautious
man, into
the person
who sees
the world in
between love
& hate, the kind
of person
that only
a payphone
could stand
talking with.

10 years
translated old country
& blues songs
into the veins
of every foot step
& thumb that
stabbed the atmosphere
when looking
for a ride.

10 years
was a 20 dollar bill
hanging out of
the thong
of every strip
club, it was
a 2 dollar whiskey
it had bought
for every dancer
named Maggie
while she brushed
her perfumed

pussy
onto its
thigh,

it was the hole
in the wall
after a night of drinking
& fighting
with one
of the many girls
it had moved in
with after knowing
them for only 2 beers,
& that hole was deep,
so deep,
that it could
see the next 10 years
as it charged out
like a midnight
freight train.

10 years
was smoking cigarette
after cigarette
from the flamingo pink
bannister of a
$125 a week hotel,
after it had borrowed
the money
to pay for it
from a distant
relative
who had already
given
up.

10 years
traded stories
with people
in the check cashing
line, while they both
sweated &
twitched out
the disbelief of

135

"this is it?"
with hall of fame
lines in their
faces.

10 years
was made out of
cardboard silver
ashtrays
that showed
the partial blur
of its face,
it was made out of
tiny plastic dixie cups
on the sink
of its hotel room
where the water
had the bitter
taste of sulfur
blanketed
in lonely nights.

10 years healed
its wounds
with poems &
unnecessary hope,
hope was never
a good friend
to 10 years, in fact,
hope had stabbed
10 years when
it just started out,
& then took off
with promise
as 10 years lay
bleeding
in the gutters
of the world.

10 years
had always been
on the loose,
its never had
anything to lose,

it had never felt
at home, but
even in the worst
of times, even
when tomorrow
felt like a constant
set of today's
& delusions,
10 years kept
burning, it
kept fighting
the empty spaces &
endless miles.

10 years always
kept shouting love
to every
piece of dust
that fell from
every ceiling fan's
repetitive heartbeat,
& it survived
for so long, only
because it learned,
quickly, how
to light up
every room
when it inhaled
that burning
red cherry
that had
always
glowed, deeply,
inside the
darkness of its
chest.

Unequaled Reaction

During those strange times,
those nights,
when my women
were out with other men,
when i could not hail a taxi,
because my pockets
were too bashful
to commit,
when the only lover
that i knew was the tree
that i was sleeping under,
when the fossil inside
my blood-knuckled heart
had to discover itself,
those were the very same
strange nights
that i discovered
how to own the world,
& it did not take much,
all i had to do
was strip down into
my underwear,
pour a drink,
light a cigarette,
open the window,
&look at the big moon,
&the brighter the moon got,
the bigger my smile,
&the closer it got to me,
the more lifelines it took,
& the more it took,
the more worlds
i knew
i would soon
conquer.

On The Road To *Damascus*

i thought about perfect places to hide,
i wanted to be blind from it all
like the children riding on the bike path,
who laugh all the way to the bottom, or
like the birds that so often take nothing,

what i got was swamps made by the rain
and they were somewhat in better shape,
better than the long distance shoes
that i was wearing to protect my thoughts,

And when i needed a break from it all
truck drivers strung out on hotel amphetamine yelled
"*your feet are wet kid...can you get outta our way
long haul to Fargo and the clock takes no prisoners*"
i felt strangely beautiful under their words,
even though my face was obsessed
by their bad teeth & old decay,

These people of fortune and powerful gods
that i watch in places you once forgot me in,
see nothing in the violence of my eyes,
they don't want to be more than conventional,
i cannot blame them for their derision,
i'd quickly close that blade too,

What i got from it was this snide laugh,
one that knows how to talk to itself
while electric fences are put up all around us,
It tries to hold onto a permanent life,
all i can see is leftover blood from its death
and the only way i knew how to beat its death
was to pack whatever rage i had inside of me
and put it into a bomb,

and watch it explode beautifully
into giant streaks of insanity
plugging the sky,

leaving death with nothing to see,
the ground up carcasses in the bunker
and the one spike that is on top of my helmet,
running back and forth,
gutting memory after memory.

The Agony of Morning

the agony of morning
sings *L'amero saro constante*
to the discarded and lonely
jack-o-lanterns
rotting in all the alley ways
and trashcans
of my heart.

The Fall

outside my window,
where the dying leaves
are falling & exposing
the skeletons of the trees,
is the only *real* truth
that i can count on
with certainty

A Family History

my doctor told me that i was young
and that my heart was in good shape,
but he wanted me on medication anyway,

he told me to take fish oil
and a baby aspirin every other day,
he told me to eat better, exercise more
and to lose some weight,

he said that i smoked too much
and that i should not binge drink,
1-2 glasses of red wine, but not 7,
1-2 beers, but not 12,

hey doc, i said, if i am in such good shape,
then what is with all of these medications?

because of your family history,
we need to be a team, you and i
and prevent any diseases,

he smiled the smile of the damned
turned around and left

as i stood up and started to put my shirt on
i looked around his office,
there were models of human brains,
the human heart,
the human lungs
and a giant picture of the human skeleton,

there was a photo of his wife
and his son
and they looked very happy
to be in the picture together,

the little boy had a puppy,
his wife had perfect white teeth
and a good enough rack
that one could rest books on it,
the picture frame that the photo sat in said "We Love You"
in bold and cursive gold lettering,

as i tried to put on one of my shoes
i had to struggle and force my foot into it,
i was too lazy to untie my laces before hand

i cursed the gods and tried
to jam my foot into the shoe a few more times
realizing that i just couldn't do it anymore,
I sat down , untied the shoe
sighed & thought

family history...what does he know!

Self-Respect

inside every agonizing set of eyes,
inside every maddening purgatory,
and inside every beautiful rose
that has ever had enough courage
to muster up the right amount of color,
is Arturo Bandini, waiting for the dust to settle
after he had just thrown a book into the desert.

Over and Over

while i watched
April's
wide-eyes,
staring at
the red headed
bartender
as she
bent over
in a short
plaid skirt
to secure her
tight
black stockings
around the
thighs
of the universe,
death
was quickly
jamming
two barrels
into his
mouth
& pulling
the trigger.

The Nowhere Kid

On those darkest and loneliest of nights
when the dog would rather growl at the shadows
than look for a bitch,
i remember how you treated me
for smoking pot and reading Dylan Thomas
in the school parking lot,

you told me that i was living up to my family name
and that soon after i was headed for a life
of *community college, 5 kids, minimum wage,*
the military, or *prison,*

i can still feel how cold the chair was that you forced me into,
the steel bolts lodged like bullets into my legs
and your hand, the one that gripped my neck,
pushed my face into an open science book,
and as i fought against you with my shoulders
you laughed like a jailer in control of the electric chair,

those minutes passed in the disguise of hours
as you gazed at me from your desk, your face
curled up like a pig standing in front of his mud bath
when you forced me to read about protons and electrons,

i was the dying mouse to your screaming hawk
when you found out that i had slipped a book of poems
in between the pages of the school book,
another no good Reardon livin' up to his name, you said
while throwing Arthur Rimbaud into the garbage,

why can't you be like the other kids you said
they're at parties, driving around town,
going out on dates, getting ready for graduation,
they're going to college, what are you going to do
...read poetry forever?

after i left, for days, months and years i roamed,
and like you said, i amounted to nothing much,
i'm poor, women have left me on the side of the road
after screwing me,
i have been in jail, i have abused drugs, been a drunk,
gone to the madhouse, been to shrinks,

searched for god and came up empty handed,

and after all your screams, horror shows and bad writing
i was never fully been able to get far enough away from you,
i remember a few years ago i ran into you
while i was drunk in a liquor store,
losing my balance in front of the cooler,
you asked me what i was doing with my life
and i said that i have been writing and not doing much else,
you looked me over, said nothing, but your eyes said *typical,*

and now, here i am, at this very moment,
its 2 am, i'm still on poverty level, still thinking about you,
and i have realized, watching the Christmas lights,
that each one of the different colors lights up
only small portions of the darkness at certain times,
sometimes, it's just the right amount of light to realize
that the farthest that i will ever need to get away from you
will be found within the words of my middle finger
as you read your students the first lines of my poetry.

Sure Fire Sound

some days
i want to open
the window
of a 70 story
building, just
so my typing
machine
has no other
choice, but
to show me
its wings.

5 Piece Meal

i.
within the empty form,
winter ends
dawn begins,

ii.
i throw the pencil into the trash,
from here on i'll speak to the mountains,
man to man.

iii.
still writing poems,
i go for a walk, hear the birds and
lose my appearance.

iv.
bears rip apart salmon flesh,
flaming poems float down
Li Po's wine river.

v.
O, cold north Atlantic,
i, too, have thrown myself upon
the edges of eternity.

They'll Gnaw Until They Find You

as i lay in bed
doing nothing but
looking through the cracks
of the blinds,

i could see the sun
and how it
kept trying
to molest
the clouds,

this is how Li Po
must have felt
while drinking wine
and he reaching
for his
reflection
in the river

this is how
Behan must
have felt after
big ass-ed women
bought
him drink after
drink, or

this is how Celine
must have felt
as he fed
his pet bird
in between
morphine induced
operations,

and when i rolled
over and
looked at the clock,
it said *1 p.m.*

instead of
getting up,

i stayed in bed,
looking out
at the clouds,

and when the
alarm
finally went
off

i could
hear the rats
as they
gnawed their
way through
my walls,

they were
looking to expose
my weaknesses,

they were
looking for a rare
flower to devour,

and as they got
closer
and closer,
i felt absolutely
nothing,

my mind was clear,
it was a good
day.

The God of War

today, i met a man
while sitting inside
the Minot mental health clinic,
he proclaimed, to everyone,
that he was "Mars, the God of War",
judging by the way he doo-wopped & sang his way
into the receptionist's candy bowl
i'd say he was dead on.

Long Overdue

he was surrounded by overdue electric bills,
overdue rent notices
& there was not even enough food
for them to eat for the next two days,

when she walked out of the bedroom
wearing fish net stockings,
high heels, see through panties
& a new bra,

she rubbed her ass on his lap
& then bent over,
slowly moving her hands up her thighs,
full white/peach ass in front of his face,
he tried to take notice of her, but
give us a 150 dollars or else occupied his mind,

she sat down on his lap,
& wrapped her arm around his neck
he did nothing but take another drag,
she rubbed her ass on his limp dick again
& he just lit another cigarette...

what is wrong with you,
you never wanna fuck me anymore she said
you're always looking at those damn past due notices,
i don't need you to fuck me every day,
but at least once a week,
come on baby, just fuck me good, just this once.

he looked at her, smashed out his cigarette & said:
you're in denial, baby, you've been getting fucked every day,
so good in fact ,that you don't even realize it.

The Same Damn Noise Is Often the Worst

night in
& night out
there are these
helicopters
& airplanes
from the base
flying above
my backyard

& they scare
away all
of the life
& i can
never hear
myself think
& the wild cats
won't come for the cans
of food
that i had left
outside
the backdoor,

& there are these
little men
inside the cockpits
& they're wearing
little helmets
on their little heads
& they're wearing
little aviator glasses
to cover up
their little faces,

i picture them
looking at little
photos of their
little blonde wives
& their little kids,
i imagine when
they're up there
that everything
is little to them,

the churches,
firehouses,
bars, cornfields,
houses, the fights,
the wars, the scandals,
the sex, the death,

i imagine, to them,
that i must be little too,
in fact, so small
& insignificant
that i am sure
they would not see me
standing next to
the last flower
on earth
as i picked it
& smelled it

even when they land
they won't see me,
they'll just smile
& wave &later on
they'll go back up
into the sky,
just so they
can make
the same
damn noise
over & over
again.

The Black Hole

it was lonely those nights in Swampscott,
out on the cat walk
where Pat and i
passed that 2nd bottle of gin
back and forth
to stop the shakes.

in the kitchen, our two women
looked like a couple of men
wearing tight vinyl pants,
and when they planned
out our night
and blew a few lines
of cocaine
it forced us to drink our gin
even quicker.

after we had finished,
we looked up
at the bright moon
and how it was surrounded
by thick dark clouds,
its brightness slowly
began to disappear from us.

and when it was all but gone
we could hear the girl/men
laughing even louder
from the kitchen,
so with all of his might
Pat threw the bottle
as hard as he could
and screamed
"Fuck you, buddy!"
and he did not stop screaming
until it was completely
engulfed
by the darkness.

"come in here you sexy guys."
the coked-up girl/men said to us.

with our heads down
we went back in.

everybody tries to have a dream
sometime,
no matter how big
the black hole gets.

Empty Handed and Losing Time
at the Poker Table of Twats

all the big shots
of the world,
who carry guns,
could never
understand
the battle cry
that comes from
a silent piece
of wind
carrying
wilted flowers
from my mantle
all the way
to the ground.

Born to Be Tamed

There are no moments for the *holy* to mumble
against the throngs of hell
when eternal nights turn up for the fight,

& it often feels that way when the mind stations itself
as the saint of the self-defeated, but

if there was ever a time,
ever a moment to absorb these cataclysms
& turn them over to the silent flowers,
that are so patiently trying to grow out from the marrow,
it would be right now, right at this moment,

pounds would shed, hidden shadows within moonlit grass,
eyes percolated & bodies of doom succumbing to bondage,

though, the torso can relate to what the mind can fever for,
there will be no sights in its paralysis
when sadomasochism yearns for a quick jerk of release,

& this is not to say that nature plays no part in aggression,
for aggression is as natural as the vigilant stars
that guide the open light between the spiked-heel & the step,

but, when wrath (cold dark & leathery wrath) needs it,
it will be on its knees like a begging abyss of agony
that seeks out its mother with never ending denial,

& those pleas for guidance, that need for humiliation,
much like powered snow blowing lifelessly in the wind;
will soon expose its backbone like the gravel road
made from the wet rock during the first of many *white outs,*

in this frenzy there are no voices, no magic words for peace,
there is only obedience & understanding,
there is only the unraveled, whether by depravity,
or a shining release that's tougher than a rebellious moan,

there are no promises, no anxiety measures,
only confidence builders & creators of fighters,
but, before the unseen pieces of the self forever vanish
like that last gasp of air before the door shuts,

there will be a strong pull upon the dog chain
that violently chokes the huge neck of the wicked.

159

Tapping The Darkness
First Thing in the Morning

while i sit in my shrink's office
drinking a cup of 99 cent
gas station coffee
she exposes her notepad

so Frank, she says,
while sipping her 4 dollar latte,
what does Francis think
of all this writing?

taking my eyes off her
miniature zen rock garden,
i bring the cheap coffee to my lips
and whisper, motherfucker,

the partially exposed skeleton
of my hand
tapping the chair's armrest.

We All Got to Eat

there's nothing
a poet can say to me
about *living*, or
truth
that a mountain range
has not already
answered.

Most Will Never Be So Lucky

when i first discovered
real solitude
they were rolling
Nana's coffin
down the aisle
of the church.

i sat to the side, alone,
and watched
men dressed in kilts
from the Police Dept.
play Amazing Grace
on the bagpipes.

there was something
in the sound
of those bagpipes
that freed me
from the rest of the people
in the church
with their loud tears,
and obnoxious bonding.

it was the perfect sound,
the perfect feeling, and
while everyone else
watched the priest
perform bullshit
ceremonies
with incense and prayer
over the coffin,

i felt a beautiful loneliness,
one that i wanted
to kiss, one
that was an electric flame
running across
the madness
of my soul.

most are never lucky enough
to feel this, or

know this, most
never want to feel this, or
know this,
they prefer large crowds,
they love the sound
of their own voice,
and they love
when people take photos
of their many faces,

but, when i finally lost
my own voice and
my own face
in the sound of those
bagpipes,
i could feel myself
rolling down the aisle
of the church,
free of it all, and
free from the need
to speak to anyone,
anymore.

Riding in a Car with S.A. Griffin

everything
was
closed up
when he
swerved
& weaved
between
the cars
with his
old brown
Volvo,

my hands,
gripping the
Jesus Christ Handles
in total panic
&
holding
it all in,

then he
stepped
on the
gas
& everything
opened
up,

like
canned
sunshine

laughter,

finally .

About the Author

Frank Reardon was born in 1974 in Boston, Massachusetts and spent his first 28 years living there. Since then, he has lived all over the country, in places such as Alabama, Kansas City and Rhode Island. He currently lives in the Badlands of North Dakota, still looking for a way to get out. Frank has been published in various reviews, journals and online zines. His first book, *Interstate Chokehold,* was published by NeoPoiesis Press in 2009. Frank is in the process of completing a third poetry collection and intends to take up additional prose/fiction writing and perhaps clay pigeon shooting.

Acknowledgements

SOME POEMS HAVE APPEARED PREVIOUSLY IN THE FOLLOWING:

Sante Fe Lit Review
Mas Tequila Review
Epic Rites
Lummox Press
Unadorned Press
Gutter Eloquence
Heroin Love Songs
Up The Staircase
Zygote In My Coffee
Unshod Quills
Durable Goods
Green Panda Press
Beat The Dust
San Antonio Lit Review

NeoPoiesis: *a new way of making*

1) in ancient Greece, poiesis referred to the process of making: creation - production - organization - formation - causation

2) a process that can be physical and spiritual, biological and intellectual, artistic and technological, material and teleological, efficient and formal

3) a means of modifying the environment and a method of organizing the self, the making of art and music and poetry, the fashioning of memory and history and philosophy, the construction of perception and expression and reality

4) an independent publisher with a steadfast goal to print and promote outstanding poets, writers and artists that reflect the creative drive and spirit of the new electronic landscape

NeoPoiesisPress.com

www.ingramcontent.com/pod-product-compliance
Lightning Source LLC
Chambersburg PA
CBHW031132090426
42738CB00008B/1060